NEW ZEALAND PAST & PRESENT

KAURI

GORDON ELL

THE BUSH PRESS

Death of a giant kauri, photographed by Tudor Collins in the 1940s. Once kauri was the characteristic tree of the forests in Northland, Auckland and Coromandel. Now only 4% of the original forests remain.

Pictures by Tudor Collins from the collection of the Auckland Museum Library.

Kauri logs stored behind a kauri dam. Such stockpiles of timber were built up above and below wooden dams in the high hills. When the dam was released, logs surged downstream to be milled. A photographic sequence of a dam burst appears on pages 18 & 19.

Tudor Collins, who took both the pictures on these pages, was himself a kauri bushman. His photographs document the tall trees and the methods used to extract them. Collins sometimes processed his glass negatives in a mountain creek and told of losing some to the resident freshwater crayfish.

The Lost Forests

Two hundred years ago much of the warmer north of New Zealand was a wilderness above which soared the giant kauri trees. The still impressive remnants of these forests represent less than 4 percent of a forest system which early last century extended north from the Waikato and Bay of Plenty through the Auckland isthmus to the Far North. The exploitation of the kauri forests and the mining of the gum they produced shaped the development of Northland, of Coromandel and the environs of Auckland for well over a century.

It was for kauri spars for sailing ships that early traders came to these coasts in the 1790s. Shipbuilders and timber millers formed many of the first European settlements in the regions where kauri grows. Gumdiggers probing for the buried resin of lost forests and bleeding the living trees for gum provided the second wave of European settlers in the northern regions. Here is an account of the nature of kauri forests and their human history, particularly over the past 200 years.

Charles Heaphy's picture View of the Kahukahu Hokianga River *(above) shows a logging operation in 1839. The small boat manoeuvres a raft of kauri logs. The timber structure behind supports a ship under construction. This picture was long thought to illustrate the yards at Horeke, originally settled as Deptford in 1826 , but it is now believed to be an early picture of Kohukohu across the Hokianga Harbour.*

Kauri Forest, Wairoa River *(left) is another Heaphy painting depicting a milling camp on the northern Kaipara Harbour in 1838. The region has few kauri now but was the centre of a flourishing export trade and of shipbuilding until the 1910s.*

ALEXANDER TURNBULL LIBRARY.

200 Years Ago

Among the first Europeans to work in New Zealand were the shipbuilders and kauri millers of the north. From the late 1790s British naval supply vessels called at the Firth of Thames to obtain spars.

Naval store ships sometimes visited New Zealand after leaving convicts at Sydney. Thus HMS *Dromedary* loaded kauri in Northland harbours in the 1820s seeking to backload spars to British dockyards. HMS *Coromandel* gave her name to one of the kauri regions following visits there, also in the 1820s.

Shipbuilding began at Horeke, on the Hokianga Harbour, in 1826. The first vessel was a 40-ton schooner called *Enterprise,* launched in 1827. Next was a 140-ton brig the *New Zealander* which had a Maori chief carved as a figurehead.

Charles Heaphy, draughtsman to the New Zealand Company, documented the new industry in these paintings dating from 1839. At left, timbermen have raised a trunk on a tall trestle, for "pit-sawing" into planks. One sawyer stood above the log, the other pulled the saw downward from below.

PROTECTED

Stationary steam haulers and bush railways were other ways of getting kauri out of the hills. While many kauri patches were too small or isolated to warrant their own railways, there were permanent bush lines serving denser stands, such as in the Kauaerenga Valley of Coromandel, the Piha and Whatipu valleys of the Waitakere Ranges on the Auckland west coast, and the kauri forests of Puketi-Omahuta in Northland. In 1910 this train ran 25km from Puketi to the Kerikeri river in the Bay of Islands, from where logs could be floated to the Auckland mill.
AUCKLAND MUSEUM LIBRARY.

The Timber Industry

The trade in masts and spars soon exhausted the tallest kauri growing along the harbour arms of the north. Then millers began felling the forests which spread far inland onto the high ridges of Northland, Auckland and Coromandel. These trees became the resource of a huge industry in kauri boards and framing.

In the 1840s water-powered mills and steam-driven saws replaced the man-power of pit sawyers at the larger mills. From the 1850s mechanisation greatly boosted output until the industry reached its peak in 1906. Fire and felling then rapidly exhausted the remaining resource. By 1930 production was only 5 percent of that peak year and by the late 1940s only 0.005 percent. Now special permission is needed to fell any trees on private land and the bulk of the remaining kauri is in public reserves.

During the 1920s, crawler tractors and heavy lorries succeeded the bullocks. Tudor Collins photographed this single-cab Leyland hauling kauri in the countryside just north of Auckland.
AUCKLAND MUSEUM LIBRARY.

Bullocks were first used to haul huge kauri logs from the bush in 1820, when a team was brought to New Zealand aboard HMS Dromedary. *It still took 10 months to procure a shipload of some 120 spars. Until the 1920s teams of yoked bullocks were frequently used to slide the giant logs through the forests. At left, a bullock team is lined up beneath a mature kauri tree in Northland in 1913.*
AUCKLAND MUSEUM LIBRARY.

The Growing Tree

Kauri takes a long time to mature and some of the forest giants exceed 1000 years old. The seedling kauri grows to maturity in two stages. For the first one hundred years or so, the tree grows rapidly, perhaps 30cm or one foot a year. In this "ricker" phase, it is thin and tall but with many side branches. In maturing, the kauri sheds these lower branches and develops a clean trunk with a "crown" of upper branches. The tree may take another two or three hundred years to mature fully.

A young kauri, perhaps four or five years old. In a favourable position it will grow quite quickly, for the next 100 years or so, adding side branches as it grows.

The kauri tree cone is fertilised by a male catkin borne on the same branch. Many seeds are scattered but few take root.

Top: Much of the surviving kauri is found on ridges like this, standing above the other species growing in the valley. These young trees are beginning to lose their side branches and develop the heavy heads which crown the mature trees. This change takes place some 100-125 years after seeding but it may be 200 to 300 years more before the trees are fully mature.

Right: The unusual sight of a young kauri, standing alone in pasture near Warkworth, demonstrates clearly the form of the "ricker". For its first hundred or so years the kauri grows at an annual rate of around 30cm (one foot) a year. When this tree matures, the side branches will drop away and larger branches will crown the clean bole of the mature tree.

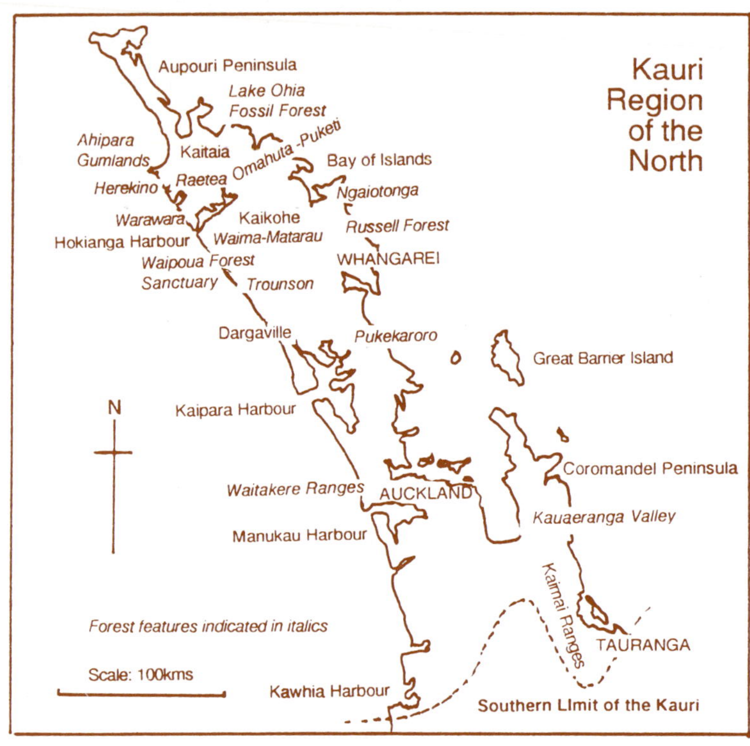

The natural habitat of kauri is in the northern North Island, defined by a boundary line south of Auckland, which takes in the lower Waikato, Coromandel and western Bay of Plenty hills. The area is home of a number of other trees peculiar to warmer New Zealand, including pohutukawa and mangrove. Specimens of young kauri have been grown successfully, however, as far south as Stewart Island, but only as a botanical curiosity. New Zealand kauri is the largest and strongest of the tropical Agathis *family, also found in Malaysia, the Celebes, New Caledonia, Indonesia, the Solomons, Queensland, and Fiji.*

Kauri Forests

The loss of the kauri forests has changed the north forever. Tall forests and swamps which once clothed the region north of Waikato have been turned to towns, cities, farms and pine forests in just 200 years.

Kauri is a form of ancient pine bearing male and female cones each spring. The family of kauri trees grows in a broad band down the western Pacific rim from Malaysia and Indonesia. The New Zealand species *Agathis australis* is said to be the finest timber variety among the 13 Agathis relatives.

In New Zealand, the kauri forest is actually a mixture of trees. While kauri are found occasionally in close stands, generally they occur in patches, often on sunny ridges, in a forest composed of several tree species. Look for the broad-spreading heads of kauri rising above the forest canopy.

While the immediate surrounds of the kauri may include the distinctive kauri grass, kiekie vine and *Dracophyllum* grass trees, the forest has much more variety than the southern beech forests which are influenced by the sub-Antarctic climate. Among the trees which grow in associations with kauri are tanekaha, the podocarp pines such as totara and rimu, rata, taraire and hard beech. This northern region of New Zealand is distinguished by its broad range of plants, often peculiar to this sub-tropical

Wood-engraver E. Mervyn Taylor depicted a breeding stalk of kauri. The smaller cones or catkins are male, the larger cone is female.

climate. These also grow among the more familiar species of the southern lowland rainforest. A lush undergrowth of vines, ferns, grass trees, orchids and small shrubs adds to the jungle atmosphere.

Moving through kauri forest can be difficult, and woodsmen tell many tales of giant trees lost and found. The latest find, a huge tree lost for several decades, was located again in the 1990s quite close to other well-known trees. Individual trees are hard to see as a whole in the dense bush. Others are infrequently visited because of their inclusion in kauri sanctuaries, declared to protect the fragile forest from casual visitors.

The search for "lost" giants during the 1960s and 1970s owed something to tales of trees like Kairaru on the slopes of Tutamoe, north of Dargaville, which had almost twice the timber volume of today's largest known tree. It was burned, as was a similar giant near Thames, late last century at a time when fire was frequently used in clearing cut-over bush.

Kauri bushland is the habitat of the large kauri snail, about 50-75mm across, belonging to the *Paryphanta* family. The largest forests have long held small populations of rare birds such as the blue-wattled kokako, kiwi, kaka and red-crowned parakeet. New Zealand's only land mammals, the short-tailed and long-tailed bats, also occur here.

The remaining forests containing kauri tend to occupy the highlands of Northland though there is substantial regrowth in the Waitakere Ranges of Auckland and in parts of the Coromandel Peninsula.

It is estimated that before the arrival of people in the north, perhaps a thousand years ago, there may have been a million hectares of kauri. Now there are just 7455 hectares of mature trees. A further 60,000 hectares of forest is said to be "regenerating". While kauri seed may be artificially planted, the remaking of an old-time kauri forest could take another thousand years.

E. Mervyn Taylor's wood engraving of Te Matua Ngahere, "Father of the Forest", was made some 40 years ago for the New Zealand Forest Service. It is still an accurate picture of a tree regarded as third only to Tane Mahuta in volume, and at 16.41 metres, considerably greater in girth. The vine at left is a rata which has taken root in the crown. Both trees can be visited along short tracks in Waipoua Forest Sanctuary, Northland.

Waipoua Stream winds through the lowland valley at the centre of the forest sanctuary. Crowns of kauri rise above the associated mixed forest. Kauri is scattered all through the 9113 hectares of Waipoua, often forming glades and crowning ridge lines.

Mature Trees

Having shed their side-branches when leaving the ricker stage, mature kauri are distinguished by their clean trunks and spreading crowns. They can take 120 years or so to assume this adult shape and can grow considerably more in height and volume for another 200-300 years. Some trees are said to have lived 1800 and more years. The crown of the mature kauri (left) comprises many branches set atop a clean trunk. Timbermen valued the clear bole (below left) which might rise 15 metres (40 feet) or more to the crown. While perching plants and vines may grow from the crown of the mature tree, the trunk itself is usually clear of such growths. This is because the tree regularly sheds its bark (below), making it difficult for other plants to get a grip on the trunk. The tree itself stands in a mound of fallen leaves and plants like kauri grass, seen at right, which protects its shallow roots. Inset photograph by Geoff Moon shows the kokako, or blue-wattled crow, a rare bird of the two largest kauri forests; also shells of the kauri snail, one of several native species which occupy the damp forest floor.

Extracting Kauri Timber

Shifting huge logs from the hillsides to the mills required special techniques. Bullock teams were used from the beginning, negotiating muddy bush trails and providing the brute force. Logs were often cut into sections to reduce the load, their ends "sniped" or roughly rounded so they slid more easily.

A journey to the mill could involve several technologies as the following pages show. Bullocks and steam haulers dragged the logs to railheads or riverbanks. Giant dams, themselves built from kauri logs, controlled water flows and provided water power to push hundreds of logs downstream. At the river mouth logs were held behind "booms" of timber in floating islands of timber awaiting the mill.

Bush camp and bullocks, pictured in the Christmas 1905 edition of the Auckland Weekly News. The carefully arranged picture shows the living quarters of the kauri bushmen, some made of timber shakes and others of nikau palm. The building at left is likely the cookhouse for it is the only one with a chimney, the large wooden structure on its right end. The bullock team has been worked off the "road", to reveal its surface, a succession of transverse logs over which the huge kauri boles were dragged.

Bullock teams drag kauri logs from a stockpile in the Northland forest. The picture is credited to Northwood Bros. Arthur, Chick and Charlie Northwood used glass plate cameras to record many aspects of life in the north at the turn of the century.
AUCKLAND MUSEUM LIBRARY.

AUCKLAND MUSEUM LIBRARY

The early timber mills on the harbours of Mahurangi, Manukau, Whangaroa and Hokianga were soon joined as milling centres by other west and east coast harbours, spectacularly the Kaipara Harbour. In the early 1900s, when the industry was centred on the Kaipara, up to 100 ships might be anchored along the northern Wairoa River picking up logs or sawn lumber. There were also mills at Great Barrier Island, and at Thames, Mercury Bay and Whangapoua on Coromandel. As extraction increased kauri logs were often towed by sea to mills on the Auckland waterfront, to be machine-sawn close to that major market and railhead. At the peak of the industry in 1906 there were 36 mills in the north, involved in cutting 443,000 cubic metres of timber.

Steam Power

Stationary engines, like the log hauler above, could be used to winch logs up steep slopes. The tiny bush locomotive beyond will take the logs out to the mill. Offcuts of timber powered these steam engines.
JOHN T. DIAMOND COLLECTION.

Traction engines, like this one preserved at the Northland Regional Museum, Maunu, were another power source in the bush.

Ruins of a kauri driving dam in the Kaiarara catchment on Great Barrier Island. This was one of three dams which could be released in succession, sustaining a strong flow of water to move hundreds of logs downstream.

Originally the framework (left) was clad with kauri boards to retain water. The logs forming the gate still swing from their retaining wires (below). This dam was last "tripped" in 1927.
Traces of dams like this can still be found in the Coromandel Ranges, the Waitakere Ranges of Auckland and in Northland.

Water Power

The earliest mechanical sawmills were powered by water wheels. Steam engines succeeded them in the 1850s, rapidly increasing production of sawn timber.
Kauri timber dams like this one, high in the hills, were built especially to move logs. Constructed from kauri timber, such dams could hold back sufficient water to create a flash flood when released. This water could "drive" hundreds of kauri trunks downstream to the sea.

This sequence of "tripping" a kauri dam combines photographs by the Northwood Brothers and Tudor Collins. Logs stacked above and below the dam are lifted up as the gate is opened, and swept downstream. Though the stream bed has been cleared of undergrowth many logs got jammed and dams were often refilled to move the logs on. Much timber was damaged as logs struck against rocks in the stream bed or tumbled over waterfalls.

Tripping the Dam

Water power was often used to shift kauri logs from the rugged hills of the north. Through summer and autumn trees were felled, often from the high ridges, then dragged and skidded down to the gorges. There the logs were stacked above and below the kauri dams. Drives were usually held in winter when there was plenty of water to move the accumulated logs. This sequence shows the tripping of a kauri dam and the frightening surge of water through the bush.

Timber was milled at the coast, or caught behind floating "booms" to be towed or shipped to mills elsewhere.

"Logs awaiting liberation by the opening of the dam." Logs held in the lake behind the dam had to be guided through the gate when water was released.

Pictures from the
AUCKLAND MUSEUM LIBRARY

Several of the greatest kauri are hidden from view in isolated sanctuaries. The Cockayne Kauri (left) in Waipoua is ranked number 20, being 10.03 metres in girth, with a trunk height of 16.33 metres and an overall height of more than 46 metres.

Toronui (below), also in Waipoua, was largest of all until it fell in 1977. It had a volume of 286.5 cubic metres but was found to be hollow. With the trampers, foreground, it now resembles a giant wooden cave.

The great timber volume of kauri can be calculated from its straight-sided, barrel-like body. Opposite top left is a giant tree from Puketi Forest. Top right is the number three tree, Te Matua Ngahere, "Father of the Forest", which is accessible by a short track from the Waipoua Forest road. The Four Sisters (bottom left) can be viewed from the same track; the trees grow so closely together that their root mounds merge so they look like one. Kauri grass (below right) grows under and around the root mounds of kauri.

The Giant Trees

Kauri is second only to the Californian Sequoia redwoods in size. Its bulk is usually estimated as a timber volume measurement, combining the girth of the tree with its straight-rising bole. The height of clean timber to the crown of branches varies, the record being 30.5 metres (100 feet). Some trees are much shorter but have tremendous girth. Overall height can reach 75 metres, well over 200 feet.

Shipping the Kauri

Many of the great harbours of the north and Coromandel had their own mills. As the kauri industry grew, further timber was taken to Auckland where the major suppliers had mills. The scow *Moa* (above) was typical of the boats which carried logs and timber about the northern coasts. These flat-bottomed vessels, built of kauri, were sailed as far as Australia with loads of timber. The largest, *Zingara*, was nearly 40 metres long, a three-masted topsail schooner scow built in 1906 and trading across the Tasman. At left, the paddle-steamer *Lyttelton* hauls a raft of logs from Great Barrier into the wharves of the Freemans Bay mills about 1930.

On the Auckland West Coast, timber from the Waitakere Ranges was hauled by bush locomotive along a coastal railway which can still be traced today. The line ended at a wharf under the giant Paratutu Rock (top right) at the north head of the Manukau Harbour. Ships from the west coast harbours, including Kaipara further north, often traded their timber direct to Australia. The stacks of kauri timber on this Auckland wharf (bottom right) are backed by a skyline of typical pioneer houses built last century from kauri.

Old Government Buildings in Wellington is often described as "the largest wooden building in the southern hemisphere". Framed in native rimu and Tasmanian blackwood, it is clad in kauri cut to resemble stonework in the classic style. Opened in 1876, the building is more than 9400 square metres in floor area. Once the home of the pioneer public service it now houses the law school of Victoria University.

Building with Kauri

Most of the houses built in the Auckland region last century were made from kauri. So too were many of the buildings elsewhere in New Zealand. During the boom in kauri felling, ships also left the kauri ports of the north direct for Australia and even North America loaded with construction timber. Some was exported to Britain and China.

The uses of kauri were many and varied, including wharves and bridges, furniture making, coachwork on railway wagons, as roof tiles and wooden pavements, and as mining pit props. Because the wood did not taint food it was used in making butter churns.

The advantages of kauri lay in its workability. It produced great lengths of clean timber, each tree providing enough for three or four houses. Kauri requires no special treatment, resisting damp and borer insects alike. The timber is also flexible and light, its grain straight and even.

Of the timber used today most is recycled from old buildings still sound after a century. Other timber, known as swamp kauri, has been carefully recovered and dried from lost forests buried thousands of years ago. This swamp kauri with its rich dark hues is used in furniture manufacture, as is much of the recycled timber.

The trickle of new timber, from private forests, commands extremely high prices and is used largely in boat building. From earliest times kauri was used in shipbuilding and many of the older workboats, launches and yachts still on the New Zealand coast are skinned in kauri.

Kauri cottages in the distinctive New Zealand colonial style are still sound homes after more than a century.

Northern Maori carved kauri for war canoes though totara was easier to work. This canoe was carved to mark the centenary of New Zealand in 1940 and is housed in the grounds of the Treaty House at Waitangi, Bay of Islands. Maori also made use of kauri gum, using it to chew and as a scent. Burnt gum produced a black ash which was mixed with shark oil to form a pigment for tattooing.

Kemp House at Kerikeri, Bay of Islands, is the oldest building in New Zealand. It was built from kauri by missionaries in 1819.

The resin produced by the kauri tree last century became the basis of another industry, the extraction of kauri gum. Gum diggers probed the swamps and wastelands of the north in search of the fossil resin from kauri trees.

The Gumdiggers

At the end of a long day, lumps of gum were laboriously scraped clean for market. The industry began in the 1840s but its heyday was in the 1890s-1910 before gum was replaced by synthetics.

Work on the gumfields was heavy, digging for buried nuggets of gum. The work attracted immigrants, including many from Dalmatia, on the Adriatic coast of what is now Croatia. By 1900 there were 5000 "Dallies" on the gumfields. Many stayed on to pioneer the wine industry in New Zealand.

A gum-sorting store in Auckland about 1906. Kauri gum was the largest export from Auckland, ahead of wool, gold and kauri timber, in the 50 years to 1900. Initially the market demanded gum nuggets which were used in the manufacture of varnishes and some paints. In the 1910s a new market developed for the poorer grades of softer gum and chips, for the manufacture of linoleum.

Crated kauri gum awaits shipment on the Auckland wharves. Packed in heart kauri crates this gum was destined for a major market in North America. Britain was the other large market, though some was then shipped on to western Europe.

All pictures courtesy of AUCKLAND MUSEUM LIBRARY.

Above: Gumland, Lake Ohia.
Below: Polished kauri gum.

MATAKOHE KAURI MUSEUM

The Gumlands

Bleak swamps and wastelands often marked the site of vanished kauri forests. Here, where kauri forests grew in prehistoric times, lay rich deposits of resin. The gathering of kauri gum began with surface collecting by Maori in the 1830-40s. Later gumdiggers probed underground for nuggets of kauri gum, testing first with a gum spear then digging down as much as five metres to the level of the "fossil" forests.

The best grades of kauri gum came from the drier hillsides, cleared of their forests during Maori times. This harder gum was preferred for making high-quality varnishes. In the peak year of 1910, more than 10,000 tons was exported. The swamp grades, often crumbly, were later found most useful in making linoleum, giving the industry a new impetus in the 1910s. While both markets eventually collapsed, with the replacement of gum by synthetics in the 1930s, a remnant industry continued into the 1950s with a few old-timers working on into the 1970s.

Several isolated parts of Northland and Coromandel were centres of gum-digging at the turn of last century, with gum-buying stores, dance halls and post offices serving perhaps a thousand diggers on a single gumfield. For the farmers who followed, digging gum on their own land was often a better source of cash than farm produce.

Gum bleeds from the stump of a kauri branch removed by a tree surgeon. Some "diggers" climbed trees for quality gum in the crown, some "bled" living trees, causing so much damage that the practice was banned in 1905.

Stumps of ancient kauri at Lake Ohia in Northland, flattened by a cataclysm 30,000 years ago. In some parts of the north the remains of ancient kauri occur in layers, dating back 100,000 years, and indicating how forest has succeeded forest over the millenia. Some "fossil forests" can still produce valuable timber. Ancient kauri, dug up and carefully dried, is known as swamp kauri and used in making fine furniture.

Kauri forest once grew on this bleak plateau neat Kaitaia in Northland. Little now grows on these white soils, exhausted by the vanished forest. Now preserved as the Ahipara Gumland Historic Reserve, the area was still worked in the 1960s.

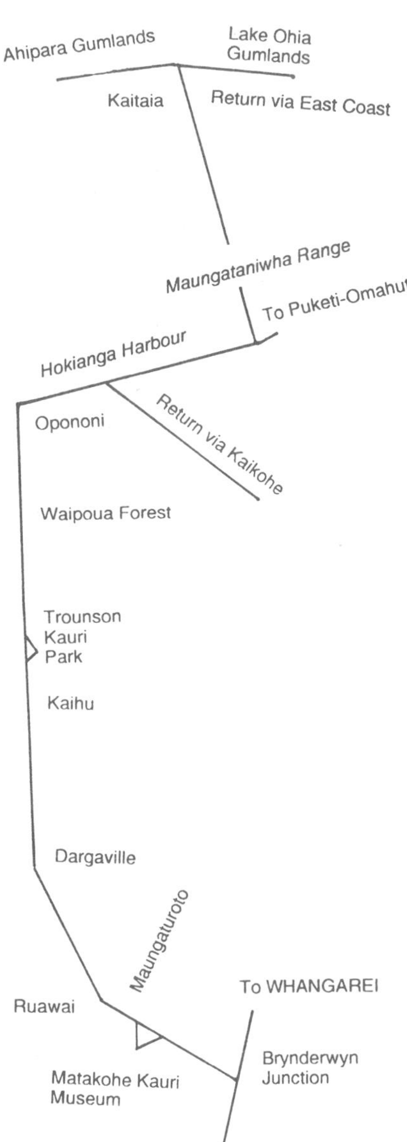

WEST COAST ROUTES

Turn west from State Highway One at Brynderwyn and cross to Dargaville and the "kauri coast". Follow the southern shore of the Hokianga Harbour inland, then choose either to continue the loop journey northward, or take the short cut back via Kaikohe.

Seeing the Kauri

While kauri forests today are but remnants of the past, there are plenty of opportunities to visit the forests. In Auckland there are kauri reserves within the city itself, notably in Northcote and Birkenhead on the North Shore. In the Waitakere Ranges along the west coast of the city are several parks containing kauri, notably the Cascades Kauri Park. The Arataki Visitor Centre has well-developed walks through typical northern bush, culminating in a fine grove of kauri.

On Coromandel Peninsula a number of small kauri remnants are preserved in the forest park but the walk in is generally rugged and trees are more easily observed as an occasional landscape feature from the road.

The broadest extent of kauri, however, lies in Northland. While small stands of trees may be seen from the road on the way north, the most substantial forests are concentrated along the "kauri coast" north of Dargaville and into the Hokianga region. Efforts to establish a Northland kauri national park have focussed on the kauri forests of this region.

The Kauri Trail

Going north from Auckland, the traveller can see two large specimen trees at Parry Kauri Park at Warkworth opposite a local history museum. Beyond Kaiwaka the whole hilltop of Pukekaroro (143 ha) is crowned with fresh young trees. Turning left at Brynderwyn and crossing to the west coast forests there is firstly the superb Matakohe Kauri Museum. Its displays of kauri timber days and gumdiggers are a fine start to a tour of the kauri country. A further museum at Dargaville traces the story of that kauri timber town and the great shipbuilding and timber export days of northern Wairoa.

It is mostly pine forest now along the slopes of the Tutamoe Range, north of Dargaville, but Trounson Kauri Park (573ha) on a side road is a magnificent remnant of mature, dense kauri trees. The main road then winds through Waipoua Forest Sanctuary (9113ha) which is the greatest remnant of mature kauri, where huge trees overhang the highway. There is an information centre and short walks to view the largest and second-largest surviving kauri trees, Tane Mahuta and Te Matua Ngahere.

Waipoua merges into the Matarau and Waima forests along the southern shores of the Hokianga Harbour. Forests containing substantial kauri also extend along the mountainous background to the northern shores of Hokianga Harbour, running almost across the peninsula of

Northland to the Puketi and Omahuta forests. Cross the Mangamuka Range to Kaitaia and there is access to the Ahipara Historic Gumlands Reserve, pictured on page 29, an apparent wasteland on a plateau overlooking the Tasman Sea at the foot of Ninety Mile Beach. Again there is a good museum of local history in Kaitaia.

The tourist can make a round trip back down the east coast, calling first at Lake Ohia (pages 28-29) at the isthmus of Karekare Peninsula, where the remains of a fossil forest dating back 30,000 years can be seen rising from the swamp. The journey southward to the Bay of Islands passes close to a number of old kauri ports, including picturesque Mangonui, the sawmilling and shipbuilding port of Totara North on the Whangaroa, and significant forest reserves such as Ranfurly Bay and Manginangina.

A detour to the south of the Bay of Islands, by way of the Opua car ferry, takes in the winding old route over the Ngaiotonga Range and passes other kauri reserves in Russell forest, as the road winds south along the remote east coast.

For a leisurely round trip from Auckland stay overnight at Opononi and somewhere on the east coast. To see the best and most accessible places quickly, drive up the west coast to the Hokianga Harbour and back by way of Kaikohe and State Highway 1.

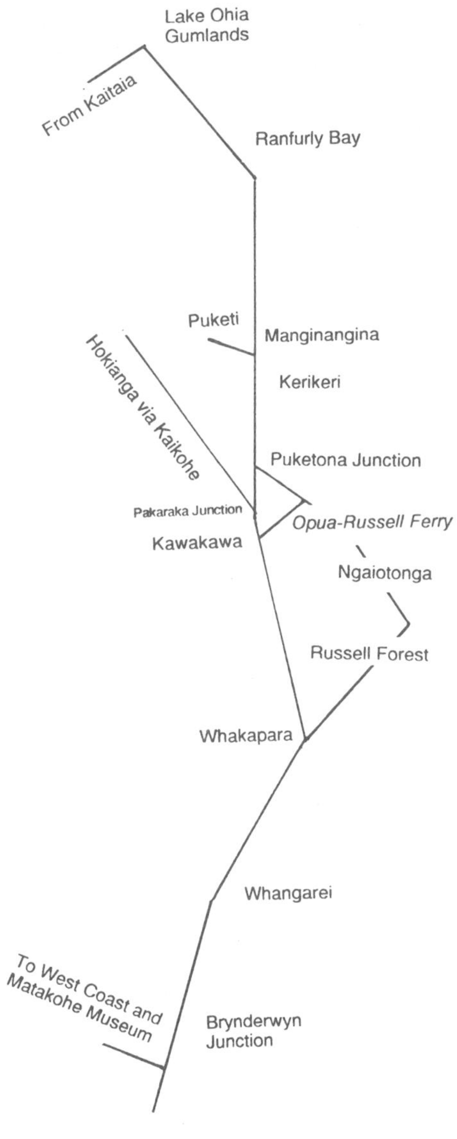

EAST COAST ROUTES
Turn off the main highways to visit kauri forests and old timber towns. Use a large scale touring map to find the best routes into old towns and kauri reserves.

Matakohe Kauri Museum

Arguably the best pioneer museum in New Zealand, the Matakohe Kauri Museum is a treasure house of Northland's European history. Its collections of equipment and displays of kauri milling and gumdigging draw thousands of visitors annually, including the bus tours of Northland's highlights. The museum is located on a hilltop about a kilometre from the main road between Brynderwyn Junction and Maungaturoto, on the road across the island to Dargaville. A small church commemorates the birthplace of Gordon Coates, Prime Minister of New Zealand in the 1920s. Part of the purpose-built museum takes the form of a large kauri country house. Its displays recreate life on the gumfields, milling equipment and a vast collection of kauri gum treasures, including carvings by the diggers and insects preserved in amber. There is also fine kauri furniture and historic tableaux of life in a kauri homestead. Other good regional museums with local perspectives on kauri, shipping and gumdigging are at Dargaville, Kaitaia, Houhoura (in the Far North) and at Maunu near Whangarei. The Historic Places Trust has several kauri buildings in its care in Northland.

A skyline of healthy kauri tops this ridge in Cascade Kauri Park, an Auckland regional reserve off the Swanson to Bethells road in the Waitakere Ranges. The slopes below are occupied with other rainforest trees.

The Auckland regional parks service offers several well-developed walks to discover the nature of the kauri, both here and from the Arataki Visitor Centre on the Scenic Drive atop the Waitakeres. Emergent kauri like this are a growing feature of many walks in the Waitakere Ranges as nature begins to repair the damage of pioneering times.

The Simpson Kauri, smaller of two big kauri trees at Parry Kauri Park, preserved as a memorial to kauri bushmen at Warkworth, north of Auckland.